THE ABSOLUTE TRUTH ABOUT TITHING

CHURCH TRADITION VS. BIBLICAL HISTORY

By

Rev. Dr. Rafielle E. Usher

First Edition

© 2010 O.M.I. Global Outreach

Unless otherwise indicated, all Scriptures marked (KJV) are taken from the King James Version of the Holy Bible. Scripture marked (NKJV) are taken from the New King James Version®. Copyright © 1982 by Thomas Nelson. Used by permission. All rights reserved. The "NIV" and "New International Version" are trademarks registered in the United States Patent and Trademark Office by Biblica, Inc.™ Scriptures marked (RV) are from the Reina-Valera © 1960 Bible Societies in Latin America © renewed 1988 United Bible Societies. Used with permission. Words that are italicized have been diligently translated from the original Greek to ensure their accuracy in meaning.

Authored by Rev. Dr. Rafielle E. Usher

Published by:

One Mission Inc. Global Outreach
13245 Atlantic Blvd
Suite 4-233
Jacksonville, Florida 32225

Future Edition Guarantee
If we release a new edition of this book, you can receive a copy at no cost. Just send us a letter with your name, mailing address, and email, and we will mail you the updated edition for free, only pay for shipping.

Visit our website for more information: https://omiglobal.org

Email: comments@DoctorUsher.com

All Rights Reserved

No part of this book may be copied, stored, reproduced, or transmitted in any form or by any means without prior permission from the author.

Table of Contents

The Traditional View vs. The Biblical View 1
The Origin of the Tithe 5
Tithing Under the Law 9
Understanding The Curse of Malachi 13
Tithing in the New Testament 17
The Origins of Modern Tithing Tradition 21
Jewish Law and Church Tithing 25
The Heart of the Matter 29

Preface

The subject of tithing has stirred strong emotions within the Christian community for many years. Some books approach this topic with the intention of confronting the church in ways that create controversy or division. Others attempt to reinforce tithing by appealing to guilt or fear. Both approaches often leave believers uncertain, frustrated, or discouraged. That is not the purpose of this work.

The Absolute Truth About Tithing was written to provide clarity rather than conflict. It does not seek to attack churches, undermine ministries, or provoke debate. Nor does it attempt to pressure readers into a particular style of giving. Instead, this book offers a careful study of the historical, theological, and hermeneutical foundations of tithing so that believers can understand the subject with confidence and peace.

The pages that follow examine three major sources: the practices of ancient cultures, the biblical interpretation and implementation across both Old and New Testaments, and the development of church tradition. By presenting these elements side by side, the goal is to give readers a complete and accurate picture of how tithing emerged, how it functioned, and how it changed over time. This book does not rely on fear based teaching or emotional manipulation. It relies on verifiable research, sound interpretation, and a sincere desire to handle the Word of God with integrity.

Many Christians simply want to know the truth so they can honor God without confusion or pressure. For this reason, the information in this book is presented with clarity and without hostility. It aims to strengthen believers, support pastors and teachers, and encourage thoughtful study rather than suspicion or division. If this book accomplishes anything, I hope it brings assurance that the topic of tithing can be understood, discussed, and practiced in a way that reflects both biblical truth and academic excellence.

May the reader find these pages to be concise, well researched, and genuinely helpful as they seek God's wisdom in their own giving.

Chapter 1

The Traditional View vs. The Biblical View

Tithing has occupied a central place in conversations about faith, stewardship, and responsibility for generations. It is a topic that inspires confidence in some and discomfort in others. For many believers the practice feels as old as the church itself. It has become a routine expression of devotion and obedience. For others the subject is covered in uncertainty. They wonder where the practice began and whether the church is teaching what Scripture truly says. Whenever conversations about tithing arise these two perspectives appear. One perspective is shaped by church tradition. The other is shaped by biblical truth. Understanding the difference is essential for every pastor and every student of ministry.

This book is not an attack on church tradition. Tradition has shaped Christian worship and community in countless positive ways. It has passed down hymns, liturgies, and practices that have preserved faith through centuries. However tradition is not the same thing as Scripture. When the two are placed side by side they must be examined with care. Throughout history some have reacted harshly to church tradition regarding tithing. They see themselves as crusaders on a mission to expose wrongdoing. They use hostile language and create unnecessary division. That is not my approach and I ask that the reader never confuse this study with such attitudes. I have no interest in joining the ranks of those who shout louder than they study. I do not share their spirit or their methods.

This book is written for academic purposes and for the training of leaders. My calling includes preparing pastors and ministers who will stand before congregations with confidence in what they teach. Leaders must handle Scripture with precision and honesty. They must be able to distinguish between what the Bible actually says and what people assume it says. For that reason we must examine the subject of tithing through a clear biblical lens. We must allow the text to speak for itself. A pastor who teaches without accuracy may unintentionally mislead the very people he seeks to serve. My hope is that this work equips men and women of God with the knowledge needed to avoid that mistake.

The responsibility of applying the information in this book rests entirely with the reader. Once the truth is presented each believer must choose how they will respond. I do not dictate how churches must structure their giving practices nor do I attempt to influence the policies of congregations. My goal is not to reshape modern church governance. My goal is much simpler. I intend to explain what the Bible defines as a tithe and how the tithe was implemented in the biblical context. If someone decides to maintain current practices that is their decision. If someone chooses to re evaluate those practices that is also their decision. Scripture supplies the facts. The reader supplies the response.

To accomplish this study we will examine the tithing passages found in both the Old and New Testaments using the King James Version and the New King James Version. These two translations provide a careful balance between literary beauty and textual reliability. They allow us to follow the language as closely as possible while still understanding the meaning in clear English. As we progress we will observe how tithing functioned among the people of Israel and how it changed through various periods of their history. We will also examine what Jesus, the apostles, and the early church taught on the matter.

By exploring the difference between church tradition and biblical truth we prepare ourselves for a deeper understanding of God's intent. Tradition may have a voice, but Scripture has the final word. Through careful study we will discover the absolute truth about tithing and allow that truth to guide our understanding moving forward.

Chapter 2

The Origin of the Tithe

As we move into the heart of our study we must begin where any careful investigation should begin. We must look at the origin of the practice itself. If we are going to separate tradition from Scripture then we must first understand where the practice of tithing came from and how it entered the life of God's people. This chapter will serve as a bridge that connects the two perspectives outlined earlier with the historical and biblical foundation on which the rest of this study will stand.

The occurrence of tithing in ancient civilizations

Many believers assume that tithing began with Israel. They picture Moses, the Law, and the Levitical system as the birthplace of the tithe. Yet history offers a broader picture. Long before the nation of Israel existed ancient civilizations practiced a form of giving that resembled the tithe. Scholars who have examined the societies of the ancient Near East have noted that several cultures used a system in which a tenth of produce, wealth, or goods was presented to rulers or temples. Van De Mieroop (2016) explains that the people of Mesopotamia participated in offerings that included fixed portions of their goods which functioned as a type of mandated tribute. Dandamayev (1992) offers a similar observation when he describes how the temples and state institutions in ancient Babylonia collected set portions of goods that supported both civic and religious structures. These findings suggest that the idea of dedicating a tenth of one's increase was known long before the formation of Israel.

This broader history does not diminish the biblical account. Instead it shows that God worked within a world where the concept of giving a tenth was already familiar. When we reach the early pages of the Old Testament we encounter the Hebrew word maaser. This word means one tenth. It is the term used throughout the Old Testament to describe the tithe. The presence of this word sets the stage for how Israel would later use the tithe within its covenant structure. Before the Law was given however Scripture presents the earliest biblical example of a tithe in the life of Abraham.

The Abrahamic Tithe

Genesis records the story of Abraham returning from his victory over Chedorlaomer and the kings who were allied with him. He encounters Melchizedek the priest of the Most High God. The passage states, "And blessed be the most high God, which hath delivered thine enemies into thy hand. And he gave him tithes of all" (Genesis 14:20 KJV). This moment is significant because it reveals the first recorded tithe in the Bible. Yet several facts must be understood with care.

Abraham's tithe was entirely voluntary. There was no command from God that required Abraham to give a tenth. There was no law. There was no covenantal instruction. Abraham made a personal choice to honor the priest of God with a portion of the spoils he recovered in battle. His act was an expression of gratitude. It was not an obligation. This detail is crucial because it stands in clear contrast to later teachings that claim Abraham tithed as part of a required spiritual law.

Another important fact is that Abraham did not become wealthy because he tithed. Prosperity teachers often claim that Abraham's tithe opened the door to his wealth. Scripture says something different. Abraham was already wealthy long before he encountered Melchizedek. Genesis 12:5 records, "And Abram took Sarai his wife, and Lot his brother's son, and all their substance that they had gathered, and the souls that they had gotten in Haran. And they went forth to go into the land of Canaan. And into the land of Canaan they came" (KJV). His resources existed before the battle and before the tithe. The tithe did not create his blessing.

A final observation is often overlooked. The Bible only records Abraham paying a tithe once. There is no verse that shows him giving a tithe again at any point in his life. Scripture is silent on any ongoing pattern of tithing for Abraham. This silence matters because it challenges assumptions that Abraham lived under a constant law of tithing. Instead the text presents a single voluntary act without any indication that he repeated it.

Understanding these truths prepares us for the chapters ahead. The tithe did not begin as a command. It did not function as a pathway to wealth for Abraham. It did not appear as a repeated practice in his life. As we continue this study we will examine how the tithe developed later in Israel's history and how its meaning changed once it became part of the covenant law.

Chapter 3

Tithing Under the Law

As we move forward from the life of Abraham into the formation of Israel as a nation, we must pay careful attention to how the tithe changes once the people enter the land that God promised them. The previous chapter explained that Abraham's tithe was voluntary, singular, and never commanded by God. But once Israel becomes a covenant nation under Moses, the tithe is no longer an optional act of devotion. It becomes a structured requirement with precise instructions. This shift marks the beginning of tithing under the Law. It also reveals that the tithe of Israel not the same practice as Abraham's act of gratitude.

When the children of Israel entered the land of Canaan, God gave them agricultural laws that governed how they were to honor Him with their increase. The tithe now became part of that legal structure. It is important to establish a crucial fact at the very beginning. According to the Law of Moses the tithe was never money. The people of Israel had money during this time period. They used currency for trade and commerce. Yet every time Scripture speaks of the tithe under the Law it refers only to agricultural produce and livestock. Grain. Wine. Oil. Herd animals. These were the items that God identified as tithe. Money was used for offerings or for the exchange of goods, but the tithe itself was never equated with money. This distinction is important because many Christians confuse tithes with offerings. They are not the same thing. They served different purposes and followed different rules.

Scripture also reveals that Israel did not give one tithe. They gave three separate tithes. Each tithe served a different purpose and each tithe had a different recipient. Understanding these distinctions is essential if the reader hopes to grasp how the tithe operated in biblical history. Let us look at each of the three tithes one at a time.

The First Tithe: Maaser Rishon

The first tithe is introduced in Numbers 18. This tithe is called *maaser rishon* which means the *first tithe*. Its purpose was to support the Levites. The Levites were the only tribe in Israel that received no land inheritance. Their calling was to maintain the tabernacle and later the temple. Scripture says, "And, behold, I have given the children of Levi all the tenth in Israel for an inheritance, for their service which they serve, even the service of the tabernacle of the congregation" (Numbers 18:21 KJV). A few verses later the Lord repeats the instruction. "But the tithes of the children of Israel, which they offer as an heave offering unto the Lord, I have given to the Levites to inherit. Therefore I have said unto them, Among the children of Israel they shall have no inheritance" (Numbers 18:24 KJV).

The first tithe was simple. Every Israelite farmer gave one tenth of their produce and livestock to the Levites. The Levites then gave a tenth of what they received to the priests. This tithe was a system of provision for a tribe that God set apart for full time ministry. It was not an offering. It was not optional. It was an agricultural tax required by the covenant.

The Second Tithe: Maaser Sheni

The second tithe is described in Deuteronomy 14. This tithe is called *maaser sheni* which means the *second tithe*. Unlike the first tithe which supported the Levites this tithe was to be eaten by the people themselves in Jerusalem during the appointed festivals. Scripture says, "Thou shalt truly tithe all the increase of thy seed, that the field bringeth forth year by year. And thou shalt eat before the Lord thy God, in the place which he shall choose to place his name there, the tithe of thy corn, of thy wine, and of thine oil, and the firstlings of thy herds and of thy flocks. That thou mayest learn to fear the Lord thy God always" (Deuteronomy 14:22 to 23 KJV).

If the journey to Jerusalem was too far or too difficult the Law allowed a temporary conversion of the tithe into money. This was not because money was tithe. It was only a travel accommodation. The instructions continue, "Then shalt thou turn it into money and bind up the money in thine hand and shalt go unto the place which the Lord thy God shall choose. And thou shalt bestow that money for whatsoever thy soul lusteth after. For oxen or for sheep or for wine or for strong drink or for whatsoever thy soul desireth. And thou shalt eat there before the Lord thy God, and thou shalt rejoice" (Deuteronomy 14:25 to 26 KJV).

The second tithe was a celebration tithe. It was used to promote worship and fellowship in the holy city.

The Third Tithe: Maaser Ani

The third tithe is known as *maaser ani*. This means the *tithe for the poor*. This tithe was not given every year. It was given every third year. Scripture says, "At the end of three years thou shalt bring forth all the tithe of thine increase the same year and shalt lay it up within thy gates. And the Levite, because he hath no part nor inheritance with thee, and the stranger, and the fatherless, and the widow, which are within thy gates, shall come and shall eat and be satisfied. That the Lord thy God may bless thee in all the work of thine hand which thou doest" (Deuteronomy 14:28 to 29 KJV). Deuteronomy 26:12 affirms this command a second time.

This tithe had a humanitarian purpose. God designed it to care for the poor. It supported the Levite again but it also served the stranger, the orphan, and the widow. These groups were the vulnerable members of society. The tithe ensured that they had food and dignity.

One final detail deserves attention. According to the Law poor people did not tithe. They were exempt. If a person qualified as poor they were recipients of the tithe. They were never commanded to give it. This truth directly contradicts the modern teaching that every person regardless of condition must tithe.

By understanding the three distinct tithes of Israel we gain a clearer picture of biblical tithing. It was agricultural. It was structured. It had specific purposes. And it served social, religious, and communal needs within the nation. As we move into the following chapters we will see how these laws shaped the life of Israel and how the tithe changes after we pass through the New Testament and move into the early church era.

Chapter 4

Understanding The Curse of Malachi

As we enter the most frequently quoted passage on tithing in modern Christian teaching, it is essential to begin where God begins. The curse in Malachi is not addressed to the congregation. It is addressed to the priests. The Lord makes this unmistakably clear at the start of chapter two. The Scripture states, "And now, O ye priests, this commandment is for you. If ye will not hear, and if ye will not lay it to heart, to give glory unto my name, saith the Lord of hosts, I will even send a curse upon you, and I will curse your blessings. Yea, I have cursed them already, because ye do not lay it to heart" (Malachi 2:1–2 KJV). These words frame the entire message that follows. God is warning the priests. He tells them that if they mishandle their responsibilities and dishonor His instructions then He will judge them. When we continue from chapter two into chapter three it becomes clear that Malachi 3 is part of this same rebuke. God is not correcting the congregation, He is confronting the priests who misused the tithe and deprived the poor of the care the Law commanded.

With this foundation in place we now turn to Malachi 3:8. The verse says, "Will a man rob God? Yet ye have robbed me. But ye say, Wherein have we robbed thee? In tithes and offerings" (KJV). The common interpretation is that the entire nation withheld tithes. Yet the context shows that it was the priests who robbed God. They received the tithes but did not distribute them as commanded. They consumed what was meant for the Levite, the widow, the fatherless, and the stranger. They turned the storehouse of God into a place of corruption. The accusation of robbery falls on the leaders who controlled the resources but refused to use them for the purpose God established.

Many teachers falsely teach that failure to pay a monetary tithe places a person under a curse. But the passage does not say that the curse comes from failing to give money. It does not even say the curse comes from failing to tithe in general. The context of Malachi is Israel's failure to obey the Law which required the people to bring the agricultural tithe into the storehouse so that the poor could be fed. The next verse helps explain this. Malachi 3:10 says, "Bring ye all the tithes into the storehouse, that there may be meat in mine house" (KJV). The word "meat" does not simply mean flesh or animal products. The Hebrew word *terep* (טֶרֶף) literally means food. God is saying, Bring the tithe so that there will literally be food in My house. This food was not for God. It was for people. It was for the poor who depended on the tithes that the nation had neglected.

When the priests misused the tithe, the poor went hungry. The curse that followed was not because the congregation failed to give money. It was because the priests failed to supply food to the needy according to God's Law. Their actions were unjust and harmful which brought divine judgment.

This theme of caring for the poor appears repeatedly throughout Scripture. Proverbs 28:27 declares, "He that giveth unto the poor shall not lack. But he that hideth his eyes shall have many a curse" (KJV). This verse connects generosity to blessing and neglect of the poor to a curse. The curse in Proverbs is not linked to failing to pay a financial tithe. It is tied to ignoring the needs of the poor. This matches the purpose of the third tithe *maaser ani,* the *tithe for the poor*, which Israel was commanded to bring every third year.

The Law of Moses reinforces this same principle in Deuteronomy 27:19. The verse says, "Cursed be he that perverteth the judgment of the stranger, fatherless, and widow. And all the people shall say, Amen" (KJV). God declares a curse on anyone who withholds justice or provision from the vulnerable members of society. Under the Law the tithes existed in part to prevent this very injustice. Therefore when Israel withheld the tithe they were not simply violating a religious rule. They were harming the poor by removing the system of provision that God put in place for them. That disobedience is what brought the curse.

Another passage that helps explain the curse in the book of Malachi is found in Zechariah 5:3. It says, "Then said he unto me, This is the curse that goeth forth over the face of the whole earth. For every one that stealeth shall be cut off as on this side according to it. And every one that sweareth shall be cut off as on that side according to it" (KJV). In this verse God teaches that stealing can cause the curse to come upon someone. Theft was a violation of the Law of God because it negatively impacted the wellbeing of others, especially the poor. So in a sense, it was considered as stealing from God because they were stealing from the people God commanded them to care for. The curse was tied to theft and injustice. It was never about a failure to give money to a religious institution.

When we read Malachi in the light of these passages the message becomes clear. The curse had nothing to do with modern teaching about tithing ten percent of income. It had everything to do with Israel's priests' refusal to use the tithe for its intended purpose. The poor were neglected. The Levites lacked support. The priest violated the covenant command to care for the vulnerable. The tithe under the Law was never meant to be used for building projects, salaries, or financial gain.

Understanding this truth frees the reader from fear and allows us to interpret Malachi correctly. The next chapters will continue to examine how the Law transitions into the New Testament and whether the tithe continues under the new covenant or is replaced with a different model of giving.

Chapter 5

Tithing in the New Testament

In the previous chapter we learned that the curse in Malachi was directed at the priests who mishandled the tithe and neglected the poor. This understanding now prepares us to move into the New Testament period where the social, religious, and economic environment of Israel begins to change. One important question must be answered. Did Jews continue to tithe during the days of Jesus and the apostles? The answer is yes, but the form of the tithe never changed. Even in the New Testament the tithe was agricultural, not monetary. Understanding this difference is essential as we compare Old Covenant tithing with New Covenant giving.

Jesus confirms that the Jews were still tithing agricultural goods in Matthew 23:23. The Scripture states, "Woe unto you, scribes and Pharisees, hypocrites. For ye pay tithe of *mint* and *anise* and *cummin*, and have omitted the weightier matters of the law, judgment, mercy, and faith. These ought ye to have done, and not to leave the other undone" (KJV). In this verse Jesus makes mention of their tithe of herbs such as mint, anise, and cumin, which are agricultural products. This proves that Jews in the New Testament continued the same system of tithing that existed under the Law. It was food based. It was connected to the Old Covenant. It was not a universal monetary system of giving placed upon all believers.

With that truth established we turn our attention to the early church. Did the Apostles command Christians to tithe? The answer is no. The Apostles introduced an entirely new system of giving that came directly from the teaching of Jesus and from the freedom of the New Covenant. The new practice was *free will giving*. The Apostle Paul explains this clearly in 2 Corinthians 9:7. Scripture says, "Every man according as he purposeth in his heart, so let him give. Not grudgingly or of necessity. For God loveth a cheerful giver" (KJV). Paul does not mention ten percent. He does not mention tithes. He does not mention any fixed number. He teaches a giving pattern that flows from the heart rather than from a legal command. The Christian gives freely because he loves God, not because he fears a curse.

In the earliest stage of the church believers practiced an even more radical form of generosity. Acts 4:32 describes this powerful unity. "And the multitude of them that believed were of one heart and of one soul. Neither said any of them that ought of the things which he possessed was his own. But they had all things common" (KJV). These believers voluntarily shared everything they had. They gave 100% of everything they owned. They were not commanded to do so by law. They were moved by love and by the presence of the Holy Spirit. This was not tithing. It was willful generosity in the earliest days of the Christian community.

As the church grew larger Paul later gave practical instructions regarding giving. He directed believers to give a portion of their financial increase for the relief of the poor. In 1 Corinthians 16:1–2 he writes, "Now concerning the collection for the saints, as I have given order to the churches of Galatia, even so do ye. Upon the first day of the week let every one of you lay by him in store, as God hath prospered him, that there be no gatherings when I come" (KJV). The key word Paul uses is the Greek word *"logia"* which means a collection for the relief of the poor. This was not a tithe. It was a charitable offering used to support believers who were suffering, especially those in Jerusalem who experienced famine and persecution.

Paul never taught that collections should be used for luxury or excess. Instead he showed by example what a minister's life should look like. In 1 Corinthians 4:11–12 he writes, "Even unto this present hour we both hunger and thirst and are naked and are buffeted and have no certain dwelling place. And labor, working with our own hands. Being reviled, we bless. Being persecuted, we suffer it" (KJV). Paul and the apostles endured poverty, persecution, and hardship. They worked with their own hands to support themselves. They did not use the offerings of the saints to fund lavish lifestyles. Their integrity stands in stark contrast to many modern abuses.

When we compare the Old Testament and the New Testament side by side the difference becomes clear. Jews continued to tithe agricultural goods during the ministry of Jesus. Yet the early church, under apostolic leadership, did not practice tithing at all. Instead they practiced free will giving as each believer purposed in his heart. They gave out of love, compassion, and obedience to the Spirit, not out of obligation to the Law. This transition marks the beginning of New Covenant giving and prepares us for the deeper study that follows in the next chapters.

Chapter 6

The Origins of Modern Church Tithing Tradition

In the previous chapter we learned that the early church did not practice tithing. The apostles taught free will giving and emphasized generosity that flowed from the heart rather than from legal obligation. As Christianity grew however and eventually became connected to political and institutional power, the practice of giving changed. This chapter will explain how tithing as we know it today did not come from Scripture but from church tradition. To understand this transition we must examine the historical records left to us by early councils and bishops.

The first question we must answer is simple. Where does our modern understanding of tithing come from? The answer is rooted in the decisions made by the early Catholic Church several centuries after the time of Christ. Historical records show that the first formal attempt to impose tithing upon Christians did not occur during the apostolic age or even during the early centuries of persecution. It began in the late sixth century.

One of the earliest references to a church wide tithe is found in the *Acts of the Bishops Assembled at the Council of Tours* in the year 567. The documents produced at this council urge believers to support the clergy through regular contributions that resembled the Jewish system of tithing. While the council did not yet require a strict tenth it laid the foundation for the mandatory tithe that would follow. According to Van de Weyer (1996) in *The Chronicles of the Early Church Councils*, the bishops encouraged systematic giving as a means of strengthening church structure and ensuring the support of the clergy.

A stronger and more direct mandate appears shortly afterward. In 585 the *Council of Maçon* issued a formal order requiring Christians to give a tithe in the same manner as ancient Israel. The canons of this council survive in historical collections. One such collection is Hefele's *A History of the Councils of the Church* (Hefele, 1895). In his summary of the council's rulings he explains that the bishops required believers to pay a tenth of their produce or income to the church. This was the first moment in Christian history when tithing became an institutional command rather than an act of free will generosity.

It is important to note that the council did not simply copy the Jewish tithe. It modified the practice in a significant way. In ancient Israel the tithe was agricultural. It consisted of grain, wine, oil, and livestock. Money was never substituted for food except in rare travel situations. However the Council of Mâcon added a new element. It taught that food could be replaced with money for the convenience of the church. This change reflected the growing administrative needs of the Catholic Church which was expanding its buildings, its clergy, and its political influence.

Several historians agree on this shift. In *The Medieval Church: A Brief History*, Wakefield (2003) notes that the substitution of money for produce was motivated by practical concerns. Food was difficult to store. Money was not. As the church grew wealthier and more organized the bishops sought a consistent and manageable stream of income to support their institutions. Tithing in monetary form became the perfect answer. Similarly, in *The Rise of Western Christendom*, Brown (2013) explains that monetary tithes became essential for the support of monasteries, schools, and expanding dioceses.

This historical development shows a clear pattern. The modern practice of monetary tithing did not originate with Jesus. It did not originate with the Apostles. It did not originate with the early persecuted church. It came from ecclesiastical decisions made more than five hundred years after the resurrection of Christ. These decisions were made to support an expanding institution, not to fulfill a biblical command.

Understanding this history helps us distinguish between biblical truth and church tradition. The next chapter will continue to explore how these traditions influenced later Christian thought and how modern churches inherited practices that the apostles never taught.

Chapter 7

Jewish Law and Church Tithing

In the previous chapter we traced the rise of monetary tithing as a church tradition beginning in the sixth century. We learned that the early Catholic councils introduced a tithe modeled loosely on the Old Testament but reshaped for financial purposes. Now we turn to an equally important question. What did Jewish law teach about the tithe during the early church period? Understanding Jewish practices is essential. Their understanding of the tithe came from their own understanding of the topic, not from later church institutions. This chapter will examine the structure of Jewish teaching during this period and compare it with the principles of the Law of Moses.

One of the most important sources for understanding post biblical Jewish law is the *Tur*, written by Jacob ben Asher in the fourteenth century. Although later than the New Testament period, the *Tur* preserves the long standing principles of rabbinic Judaism that were already present in earlier centuries. These principles reflect the understanding of tithing that existed within the Jewish community long before the church councils modified the practice. The section that addresses charitable giving is *Yoreh Deah 331*, and it provides clear guidance on the order of responsibility for supporting the poor.

In *Yoreh Deah 251:3* the instruction is straightforward. It says that a person must first secure his own livelihood before he gives tithes or charity. The text states that a man's own needs come before the needs of others. After he has secured his stability he must honor his parents if they are poor. After that he supports his adult children, then his siblings, then his extended relatives, then his neighbors, then the people of his own town, and finally the people of other towns. This progression of responsibility demonstrates a deep commitment to compassion and family obligation. It also reveals that Jewish law never forced a person into financial hardship in order to give. Wealth was not a requirement for righteousness and poverty was not a spiritual virtue. Jewish tradition explicitly rejects the idea that intentional poverty makes someone more holy. Historical summaries of Jewish ethics such as those found in the *Jewish Encyclopedia* and the scholarly articles referenced on various theological websites confirm that Judaism consistently opposed the glorification of willful poverty.

The instructions of *Yoreh Deah 251:3* also reflect the core values of the Old Testament. Scripture teaches the responsibility of caring for one's own family before others. The apostle Paul reflects this same principle when he writes, "But if any provide not for his own, and specially for those of his own house, he hath denied the faith, and is worse than an infidel" (1 Timothy 5:8 KJV). Even though Paul is writing as a Christian apostle he is applying the long established Jewish ethic that personal responsibility precedes charitable giving.

Another important point in Jewish law concerns the recipient of the tithe. Under the Law of Moses only the Levites were authorized to receive the *maaser*. Numbers 18:21 states, "And, behold, I have given the children of Levi all the tenth in Israel for an inheritance, for their service which they serve, even the service of the tabernacle of the congregation" (KJV). Jewish belief has never changed on this matter. In both ancient and modern Judaism the tithe belongs to the Levite because God gave them no land inheritance. Therefore many Jewish scholars historically argue that Christian pastors who receive tithes are in error because they are not Levites and do not fulfill the Levitical role.

This view is not merely a modern opinion. It reflects the traditional interpretation that extends from the first century until today. Rabbinic law maintains that the tithe may not be paid to anyone outside of the tribe of Levi. Scholars such as Isadore

Epstein in *The Jewish Law of Tithes* (Epstein, 1930) explain that Judaism views Christian tithing as a mistaken transfer of a covenant obligation that was never assigned to Gentile believers. The Jewish community therefore saw the early church not as a continuation of Levitical legislation but as a separate spiritual movement with its own practices. The apostles themselves never commanded tithes because they understood that the tithe belonged to a priestly class that no longer functioned after the destruction of the Temple in AD 70.

A third principle of Jewish law concerns the use of the tithe. Jewish tradition strictly prohibits using the tithe for personal luxury. The tithe was set aside for sacred purposes. It provided for the Levite, the poor, the stranger, and the widow. The Levite himself was not permitted to enrich himself with the tithe. He received only what was necessary for his survival because his duty was spiritual service, not personal gain. Historical works such as *The Jewish People in the First Century* edited by Shmuel Safrai (1976) confirm that the Levites lived modestly and often endured hardship. Extravagance was never associated with the tithe. This stands in stark contrast to modern abuses where some leaders use tithes to support lavish lifestyles. Such behavior is completely foreign to the Law of Moses and to Jewish interpretation.

A final note must be mentioned. Jewish tradition rejects the idea that deliberate poverty is a sign of righteousness. While compassion for the poor is central to Jewish law, intentional self inflicted poverty was never encouraged. Works such as *Everyman's Talmud* by Abraham Cohen (1949) explain that Judaism values responsible stewardship, honest labor, and financial stability. Poverty was a circumstance to be helped, not a badge of spiritual honor. This concept provides a sharp contrast to certain later Christian movements that glorified monastic poverty. Judaism valued generosity and compassion without encouraging asceticism.

When we place all of these teachings together a clear picture emerges. Jewish law during the early church period maintained the same principles found in the Old Testament. The tithe belonged to the Levites. The tithe was agricultural. The tithe supported the poor and the servants of the sanctuary. Giving did not begin until a person could support himself. Wealth was not sinful and poverty was not a spiritual achievement. These principles shaped the culture in which Jesus and the apostles lived. They also stand as a witness against later distortions that emerged in church tradition.

Chapter 8

The Heart of the Matter

In the previous chapter we examined Jewish law and the way it shaped the early understanding of tithing among the people of Israel. We saw that the tithe was agricultural, that it belonged to the Levites, and that giving in Jewish life always placed compassion for the poor at the center. Now we turn to a deeper spiritual question that connects the Old Testament practice of tithing with the New Testament life of grace. The writer of Hebrews gives us a powerful key for understanding how the Law functions after the coming of Jesus Christ. This key is the concept of foreshadowing.

The book of Hebrews begins chapter ten by saying, "For the law having a shadow of good things to come, and not the very image of the things, can never with those sacrifices which they offered year by year continually make the comers thereunto perfect" (Hebrews 10:1 KJV). The writer tells us that the Law was a shadow. A shadow is a real outline, but it is not the full substance. It points toward something greater. The sacrifices of the Old Covenant were not the final answer. They foreshadowed the perfect sacrifice of Christ. In the same way the tithing system of the Old Covenant served a purpose in its time. It supported the Levites and cared for the poor. Yet it was only a shadow of the greater generosity that God would reveal in the hearts of His people under the New Covenant.

When we understand the concept of foreshadowing we can begin to see the real heart of the tithing issue. It is not about whether a believer chooses to tithe or not to tithe. The New Testament never commands tithing as a requirement for salvation or blessing. Instead it reveals the deeper question. Are we giving as believers in a way that reflects the compassion and character of God? Under the Law, giving was required because it maintained the social structure of Israel. Under grace, giving flows from a transformed heart filled with love.

The first part of the heart issue is that giving is not measured by a fixed percentage. Whether a believer tithes or does not tithe is not the central concern. The real concern is whether the believer gives in a way that reflects the mercy and justice of God. Jesus reminded the Pharisees that the weightier matters of the Law were "judgment, mercy, and faith" (Matthew 23:23 KJV). When giving becomes obligatory or fear based it loses its spiritual significance. But when giving flows from a heart of compassion and mercy, it transcends into an act of worship.

The second part of the heart issue is the responsibility to care for the poor. Throughout Scripture God connects blessing with the care of the needy. Proverbs 19:17 teaches, "He that hath pity upon the poor lendeth unto the Lord. And that which he hath given will he pay him again" (KJV). This principle never changes. Whether a believer gives through a tithe, through offerings, or through simple acts of generosity, God honors the heart that remembers the poor. The Old Testament tithe was designed to support the vulnerable. The New Testament offering also carries that same concern. Paul wrote to the churches, "Only they would that we should remember the poor. The same which I also was forward to do" (Galatians 2:10 KJV). The apostle saw giving not as a requirement of law but as a joyful responsibility of love.

The third part of the heart issue is spiritual direction. A believer must pray and hear from God about how to give. The Holy Spirit guides the Christian in every area of life. Giving is no exception. When a believer prays sincerely, God will speak to the heart. He will direct the amount, the purpose, and the timing of the giving. This is why Paul wrote, "Every man according as he purposeth in his heart, so let him give. Not grudgingly or of necessity. For God loveth a cheerful giver" (2 Corinthians 9:7

KJV). Giving must not come from fear. It must not come from manipulation. It must not come from pressure. It must come from the inner purpose of the heart, shaped by prayer and guided by the Spirit of God.

This brings us to a very important conclusion. Is it wrong to tithe? The answer is no. There is no sin in tithing. A believer is free to follow church tradition if it helps structure their giving. A believer is also free to follow the apostolic teaching on free will giving. Under the New Covenant both practices are permitted. There is no curse attached to either choice. What matters is the heart behind the giving. If a believer tithes out of fear then the blessing is lost. If a believer gives freely and joyfully, whether through a tithe or through offerings, God will bless it.

The essence of giving is not the percentage. It is the purpose. It is the love behind the act. It is the desire to honor God and to care for His people. Whether through tithes, offerings, or daily acts of generosity, God responds to the heart that gives with joy.

References

Addis, W. E., & Arnold, T. (1889). *The Catholic dictionary* (6th ed.). New York: Author.

Cohen, A. (1949). *Everyman's Talmud*. New York: E. P. Dutton.

Dandamayev, M. A. (1992). State and temple in Babylonia in the first millennium BC. In M. Heltzer & E. Lipiński (Eds.), *Society and economy in the Eastern Mediterranean (c. 1500–1000 B.C.)* (pp. 248–251). Peeters.

Domb, C. (Ed.). (n.d.). *Ma'aser kesafim: Giving a tenth to charity*. Feldheim.

Epstein, I. (1930). *The Jewish law of tithes*. London: Soncino Press.

Fanning, W. (1912). Tithes. In *The Catholic encyclopedia* (Vol. 14). Robert Appleton Company. Retrieved May 26, 2011, from https://www.newadvent.org/cathen/14741b.htm

Ferraris, L. (1886). *Bibliotheca canonica* (Vol. 3). Rome: Author.

Feinstein, M. (n.d.). *Igrot Moshe* (Yoreh Deah II, 112).

Hefele, C. J. (1895). *A history of the councils of the church* (Vol. 4). Edinburgh: T. & T. Clark.

Kanievsky, Y. (n.d.). *Orchat Rabeinu* (Vol. 1, p. 302).

Kelemen, L. (n.d.). *Permission to receive*. Targum Press.

Safrai, S. (Ed.). (1976). *The Jewish people in the first century*. Assen: Van Gorcum.

Selden, J. (1618). *History of tithes*. London: Author.

Shulchan Aruch. (n.d.). *Code of Jewish Law* (Yoreh Deah 249:2).

Spelman, H. (1723). *Of tythes*. London: Author.

Tur, Jacob ben Asher. (n.d.). *Tur Yoreh Deah* (Sections 249–331).

Van De Mieroop, M. (2016). *A history of the ancient Near East, ca. 3000–323 BC* (3rd ed.). Blackwell Publishing.

Wakefield, W. (2003). *The medieval church: A brief history*. Blackwell Publishing.

Wikipedia contributors. (n.d.). *Intentional poverty in Judaism*. In *Wikipedia, The Free Encyclopedia*. Retrieved from https://www.wikipedia.org/

www.ingramcontent.com/pod-product-compliance
Lightning Source LLC
Chambersburg PA
CBHW071803040426
42446CB00012B/2687